Lost in an Idyll

Joseph Bender

ISBN: 0615763669
ISBN-13: 978-0615763668

Chapter 1

Merciful Lord supreme, empower and
Permit the muse to grant me grace and wit,
And keenly honed remembrance, that my words--
Recalling those of Paul my dad-- may shine
As street lamps light the paths of men at night,
And luminate your ways, oh Lord divine.

Upon the evening ere my voyage from
My home in Maine to Iceland and Svalbard
(We researched plants on those aloof islands:
Collecting tissue culture specimens,
We stored them in our sleek and swift sailboat,
And brought them back to analyze in depth),
My father wished me luck on my journey
And said: For your successful, safe, and fun,
Productive trip I'll pray. In arrogance,
My words then crossed their barrier (my teeth).
Replying thus, I said: No need for help

From God will stay my journey to those lands.
My father zealously rebuked my words,
As he well-knew that God swayed my unknown
And fragile fate. As sunlight faded fast,
The Moon and stars appeared, and he began
To tell a harrowing, amazing tale,
Recounting his Colombian journey,
In which he braved so many grim trials.
Enrapt I attended his tale of woe:
A tale I'll now recite, returned from my
Adventure sailing on Atlantic seas;
My dad back home in dry San Diego.

In San Diego Paul'd started to tell
His story, surfing swelling waves at Scripps,
A pier with sandbar sweet to surfers' needs.
He 'woke before the sun's refulgent rays
Could light the sky, as Venus rose above
The hills, the east aglow with saffron hints
Of sunny morn; the sun's path at its hot,
Persistent zenith. He grabbed his dripping-wet
And frigid wetsuit, pulled it on over his feet,
Then up he pulled the suit to his cold-shocked,
Bare waist (as in those hottest months the sea
Is still too cold to surf without the warmth
Of girding wetsuits), hurried to his truck,
And hastily backed down his drive; his board
Already stowed-- it wont to stay in the bed.
As Paul approached the pier, he saw the winds
Were calm, and blowing from the east. The waves

Were near head-high, and Matt his friend he saw
Alone: he-- stretching limberly by the
Pacific's lapping waves-- sat on the sand.
To join him, Paul forthwith jogged down seaward.
They paddled out together, diving deep
Beneath the chilling waves. A looming set
Neared, and as rows of soldiers march in sync,
It rolled, and silently it signaled where
Its peaks would form. To win a wave Paul strove:
He paddled hard to reach the peak of the
Third crest, and won the best position held
By any surfer; rapidly he stroked,
And kicking briefly, caught the wave behind
The peak a meter back. The crest then fell;
The shoal beneath it urged it forth with strength;
Meanwhile, with lightning-fast response he poised
Himself and simultaneously crouched,
Thus found himself enclosed within the tube,
And rode untouched for seconds long outstretched.
Exulting, Paul returned to Matt, and told
Of his fantastic ride: a ride to be
Remembered when entranced by pleasing thoughts.

Matt then began to reminisce about
His trip to Panama to surf the breaks
He'd heard of there. His words portrayed blue waves
That barrel over reefs diverse with hues
All motley, painted scenes of bright and loud
Macaws and howler monkeys moaning deep,
And told of thronging plants so lushly green.

Then, piquing Paul's attention, Matt recalled
The insects teeming there: the moths so large;
The beetles girt iridescently; ants
That owned estates by sway of force; the noise
Of crickets; nests of termites; buzzing bees.
Enthralled he listened; tumbling thoughts he tossed
About. Already, plans of traveling
Distracted him from Matt's story, which soon
Again described the pounding swells he'd surfed.

Weary and hungry, Paul and Matt rode waves
To shore. They lit a joint, enjoyed its perfume
And potency, then walked to a pizza
Parlor, where, sated they discussed the thoughts
Of Paul regarding traveling to wet
Colombia to find and classify
Unknown Lepidopterans. Matt declined
An offer Paul then proffered him, to go
With him to brave the wilderness so raw
And immense. As they set forth toward
Their homes on their own paths, (the one lived near;
The other walked truck-bound) swift thoughts of Paul's
Implacably were fixed on insects strange
And foreign: insects scientists were yet
To classify. He knew he'd soon arrange
A trip to darkly forested tropics.

Few weeks then passed before he'd scheduled flights,
And hired a guide to meet him when he'd light.
The day arrived to fly Colombia-

Bound: Paul's excitement rose as when before
A contest, fear of failure matched with hope
To win is mixed, thus stirring stout stomachs.
Excitedly he boarded the swift jet,
And soon the weight of sleep did sink his lids.
He woke as thuddingly the jet alit
Upon the runway. Down a wheeled staircase
He left the metal bird and made his way
To his next flight, Bogota's pleasant air
Cooling his lungs. Nearby a docked floatplane
Awaited him. It was a nicely kept
Cessna on floats, a 1975
Model, and only five years old at that time.
It sat ashine, all prepped and fueled to fly;
A local lake its placid mooring place.
Her pilot was a leathery old man;
Incessantly he smoked Marlboro Reds.
The midday sun burned high above tall trees,
As into'er rear the two quickly loaded
Paul's bags. They climbed aboard the shiny bird;
La Chorrera their destination. They
Then launched, and took to flight, the Caqueta
River to be their landing strip-- it near
The small, remote, and beautiful town sought
By Paul. He gazed from high on the verdure
Below, as rapidly they sped on south.
His pilot jump-started each cig he lit:
In sequence puffing down each short-lived one.
Far off, the muddy- watered river neared.
With slowing pace they lined up with her course,

And skillfully the pilot lit his craft
On calmly flowing waters brown with mud.
They moored the plane and unloaded his bags.
The rough old pilot had a stash of weed
Of highest grade, and said he'd sell an ounce:
Without delay Dad bought it happily.

The two then met the local guide who'd show
Him through the dark forest in hope to find
Unknown and fascinating moths, skippers,
And butterflies. The three ate supper, smoked
Joints, and conversed in Spanish. Leaving them,
The pilot wished them luck, and walked back to
His craft. As they sat talking, rumbles rose,
The distant sound of the swift plane's ascent.

Paul's guide-- a short, quick-eyed, thin man-- seem'd quite
Experienced, although his visage showed
No signs of aging (near twenty he looked).
His name was Tim. Like many locals, he'd
Become addicted to the tradition
Of chewing coca leaves, and was on edge:
Paranoia growing in his mind yet young.
To Paul's reserved room Tim brought him, and walked
On home, the morn and hiking on his mind.
They'd leave at dawn and hike toward Brazil.

At dewy dawn, as the sun's rosy rays
Crept up, replacing starry skies, the two
Arose to scents of coffee, birds' clamor,

And cool, refreshing breezes rustling leaves.
They met where Paul sojourned the night just passed,
Ate breakfast, spoke of hiking overland
East and southeast, then took inventory:
Their three- day trip required little food--
In Tim's unburdened pack they stowed their meals
Along with Tim's tent and his sleeping bag.
Equipment stuffed Paul's pack: kill-jars for six-
Legged specimens, encasing boxes fit
For the like, his insect net, His two-person,
Old tent and sleeping bag, and one fine ounce
Of Gold (the green, Colombian, good kind).
They each additionally brought water
Bottles, and tabs that disinfect water.
They then set off, their plan to walk to a
Tall waterfall twenty-nine miles away,
And then to turn, retracing the same paths.
In hand his Zulu-style assegai--
A hunting spear; to his old leather belt
He strapped his bowie knife: thus armed Paul walked.
Around his neck his compass hung and swayed.
All 'round them, birds of divers colors chirped,
And clucked, and sang. Here motmots flew from holes
In th'earthen hillside: plumage strange festooned
Their tails; and there quetzals did roost in trees:
A greenish blue hue their backs did show,
And lengthy plumes adorned a male's green tail.
Their chests were ruby red, and though they were
Quite hard to spot, indeed like kings well-dressed
In fine, unrivaled garb they seemed. Tall trees

That blocked the sun with thronging limbs did form
A dense and layered canopy of leaves--
So dense, the sun was scarcely seen, though clouds
Were yet to crowd the sky. On buttressed trunks
Lianas climbed, orchids abounded, bright
Bromeliads were bunched, and mosses crept
About. From Banyan trees that spread afar,
Black howler monkeys swung and bellowed groans
As though lamenting. Roots of trees did cross
The trail, and lo! beneath a root a large
Tarantula's abode he saw. They stopped,
And used a stick to lure the beast without
His hole. Enormous, hairy, black, and hissing,
He issued forth. Onward they walked, as hot
The day then waxed. Iguanas long and green,
Like stately dragons, calmly watched them near,
Then wearily would seek the thicker brush.
They saw a rattlesnake plant blooming near
The trail, and on a leaf it held a brown,
Little, and well-built nest: that of a blue
And green, tenacious hummingbird that buzzed
Around a stalk that bore the plant's stacking,
Bright-yellow blooms. A few short meters down
The trail, a black tree frog with red-orange spots
Was perched: it chirped and sang away at ease,
Unmoved as they approached-- it heedlessly
Enrapt in calling mates. The light of day
Then soon to fade, they stopped on level ground,
And started setting up their camp, when-- stoked--
Paul saw and caught a butterfly with wings

That stretched out wide; its scaly form chartreuse.
He thought it strange, and hoped it was unknown
To science. Killing it in a jar filled
With alcohol's unseen, fell fumes, he prepped
It to be pinned. He spread its wings and pinned
It in a case, delighted he'd forthwith
Found such an interesting butterfly.
The two then pitched their tents and built a pyre
Of branches, twigs and leaves (it was the dry
Season, and though at times cool rain did grace
That land, a few hot days had passed since last
It soaked the ground: well-parched the wood thus was
Which fueled their fire). His handy Zippo Paul
Employed to light some kindling wood, and flames
Engulfed the pyre. They sat conversing while
Beside the blaze they ate dinner, laughing
At funny jokes, enjoying night's cool air.

Retiring tent-ward, sleep in mind, the two
Succumbed to weary lids. As night wore on,
Reposing peacefully Paul dreamt, and morn
Did near, yet ere the morning star could rise,
Forebodingly, to his unconscious mind
With words of warning, garbed in linen cloak,
A man-- who said his name was Michael, and
That he was sent by God-- did come; he told
Him-- stern his words, and countenance austere--
To seek the succor God would grant him should
He pray with humbly suppliant appeals
For safety. Also, Michael warned they'd be

Bitten by jackals, suffer further trials
And woes, and feel bereft of hope. He woke
With thoughts of jackals: Michael's words he knew
Distinctly-- not like dreams are wont to be:
Remembered muddled-- but he thought it strange,
As jackals aren't American critters.
Thus Paul determined it was just an odd
(Albeit vivid) dream. They ate, then packed
Their tents, prepared to hike, and stood gazing:
A large and stinky mushroom stood above
The forest floor. As Paul then checked his compass,
He caught the eye of Tim, and curious,
He asked if Paul would mind him looking at
The finely wrought device. As Paul then tossed
His compass, swooping overhead a hawk
Did fly, and seized a snake, then flew away.
Forthwith, before unseen, two men-- who held
Machetes sharp-- approached and threatened Tim.
Swiftly he ran: as when a deer is chased
By dogs, and springing bounds away in haste,
His feet but barely touching ground: so ran
Young Tim, and 'lone left Paul, who grabbed his spear
And threatened death. The twain then fled apace.

Chapter 2

As Paul-- in shock-- then stood amazed, to Tim
He called, and called again, did not receive
Response, and soon he realized Tim still had
His compass. Gazing, Paul-- like hapless men
Entangled in the Minotaur's grim maze--
Did stand agape, in awe of forest thick
And vast. He thought how best to make his way
On back to La Chorrera. Dense tree
Cover, and hazy skies inhibited
His capability to navigate.
Bereft of compass, judging it most wise,
He walked retracing steps of theirs. His plan
Was soon to prove to be untrustworthy,
As rain did fall, and washed away their prints,
And then before his eyes the trail diverged
In three directions. Not unlike where three
Erosive rivers same in color come
Together, those like trails had merged, and Paul

In woe did ponder which to take, as when
He'd walked the other way, he hadn't seen
The other two acutely merging trails.
He walked about fifty yards down each trail,
And didn't see familiar sights at all.
Dismayed, instead he found that each was forked.
He thought one route did seem most fit, and trod
Along, his hopes then waning fast away.

For four distressing days he walked (and camped
For three unnerving nights) before he found
A welcoming and friendly village. There
He ate a strengthening, warm meal, and then
Before their campfire, he twisted a joint,
Lit it, and took a puff: he passed it on,
And-- calm at last-- at length began to tell
Two Spanish-speaking men his tale of those
Four days so fearful and so harsh just passed:

The fateful day they were attacked, the air
Was steaming-hot by noon (or so); the ground
Though wet that morn, had dried and leaves did crunch
Beneath his boots. The day felt long, like days
Of northern summers. Hungry, Paul desired
To find and kill some game. Before the sun
Could set, he saw a fat agouti, quite
Unheeding, sitting munching leafs just yards
Away. He cast his spear, and scored a hit:
The blade did plunge on through its back, and loosed
Its tiny limbs. Triumphantly, he grabbed

His fallen prey. He built a fire, then cut
Apart the creature, spitted its sundered
Meat, and with pleasure roasted it: the flames
Did dance and lick the cuts 'til they were browned,
And smelled of smoky scents. He gorged himself
On tasty meat, then took the rest, and far
Away from camp, flung it with bones and skin,
In hope it wouldn't lure those toothy beasts
(That lurked about the jungle there) toward
His resting place. He reared his tent aside
The coals, and-- weary-- laid to sleep within.

Forthwith he woke as soon as Phoebus lit
The land; his confidence restored to some
Degree; as feasting on that rodent gave
Him faith in his abilities. He stowed
His tent, then walked along the trail feeling
Strong; but as hours did pass, his health began
To fade, and ill he grew: a fever struck
Him down, and on the trail he sat against
A tree; his strength in short supply; his mind
Delirious. The forest seemed to ebb
And flow; its sounds were blended noise: a din
Of discord encompassed him. Briefly, thoughts
Would near completion, but then faded from
His mind. He recognized the symptoms were
Malarial, and of severe malaria
At that, but in no wise could help himself.
He fell unconscious, sprawled- out on the trail.
As sensibility returned to Paul

(At least enough that he could gaze about),
He watched a man approach, who wore a garb
Of animal skins, beaded necklaces,
A headband ringed with bright, standing feathers
Of divers shades of blue, and green flip-flops.
He was a shaman, old and wise, who knew
The healing ways of plants and moist fungi.
He sat beside sick Paul, and in a pot
Prepared an ayahuasca brew. He built
A fire, and boiled the mix: liana, leaves
And water. Pouring some for Paul, he said
A prayer, and gave him the syrupy drink.
He gulped it down, and sat there aching from
The sickness. Once again, he fell asleep,
And slept until the ayahuasca took
Effect. When he awoke, he wasn't in
This world. Instead, he found himself within
His body, marshaled with a host of fierce,
Spear- throwing, sword- wielding Leukocyte men;
Enormous, red, bifurcated caverns
Their battlefield. The commander who swayed
The host was Joshua. His armor wrought
With gold and silver, tin and bronze, he shined
With preternatural illuminance.
His greaves were tin and triple layered; gold
Did cover two layers of bronze within
His gleaming helmet, which was topped with crest
Of ruddy horsehair; silver Clad
His breastplate's bronze; his sword was hammered steel,
And studs of gold adorned its hilt; he held

A ponderous, ash spear-- its head was weighty steel
And razor sharp; his shield was skillfully
Designed-- its five bull's hide layers were topped
With one of bronze, and finally, one made
Of graven gold. The shield's imagery
Depicted crossing safely-dry amid
The parted Red Sea, and Pharaoh's hopeless
Pursuit; the ark with mercy seat of gold,
And Aaron dressed in priestly, fine garments,
Censer in hand; the rock which Moses smote
Against the will of God, when told that speech
Would spill its water forth; the twelve smooth stones
In Gilgal, brought out from the Jordan's midst;
And-- taking up the biggest space-- the downed
Ramparts of Jericho, near seven men
Who blasted trumpets of swift victory.

Encircled by a thronging mass of troops,
The stout commander stood, and when his men
Were silently intent, he spoke aloud:
Malarial soldiers invade this realm
Of ours, and threaten destruction and doom.
They aim to wipe us out and take this place.
We wound their men to scant effect: when cut,
They heal too fast-- though, cleft sunder, they die.
We've lost a great many strong men, and now
I call ye here to organize our might,
That we may crush our foes with decisive
Success. The chief of the Malarial
Legions-- Anopheles-- commands his men

With skill. Well-trained and stalwart men they are.
To win this war, we must enlist the help
Of God. I ask ye now to bow thine heads,
And join with me in prayer. Almighty God,
To us provide superior puissance,
That we may rout our foes in battle. Yea,
Our arms are of no use, without thy strength
Behind our fight. Please, bless our men, and grant
Us wisdom, that we may soon win this war.

His words were heeded well by God, who sent
To them his messenger: swift Gabriel.
He brought with him cinchona wood-- a vast
Supply-- enough to make them lengthy spears
And soaring arrows to replace all those
They now did use to no avail. At once
They got to working on the deadly shafts.
Employing all the host, the work was done
In only two short hours, and all the men
Were outfitted with new weapons of war.

In armor Paul was dressed. He held a spear
Tipped with the sharpest steel; a baldric held
His weighty sword of steel, its width adorned
With images near where it crossed his chest.
It showed his birth and happy parents' smiles;
His first good wave he surfed; him fencing with
A friend; him shooting his bow and arrow;
Him layback grinding on his skateboard; plants
Growing in garden beds; and most unique,

His dog: her image lay awaiting him
(He'd left her with a friend who cared for her)
To come back home, her ears noticeably
Turning about, in hope to hear a sound
Made by her master. Paul did wield a bronze-
Clad shield of five layers (the first four made
Of tin); its smoothly polished face ashine.
His fearsome helmet covered all but eyes
And mouth-- its cladding gold; its crest a red,
Distinctive plumage. Battle-ready, Paul
Repaired along with fellow Leukocytes
Toward the huge Aorta, where the hosts
Arrayed to fight, with horrid arms clanging.

The lines approached each other
Until within the range of arrows, stopped,
Examined the opposing ranks, and stood
Awaiting orders. Joshua summoned
His seven men who held shrill horns,
And ordered: Blare the archers' signal!
At that they blew a few sharp blasts,
And all the bowmen quickly loaded darts
Upon their weapons. Creaking all at once,
They bent their eager bows concertedly,
And to their hands drew back the barbed heads.
The trumpeters then blew another blast,
Thus raining flying death upon the ranks
Of enemy Malarial soldiers.
The flight of darts dealt widespread destruction
On the unheeding men, who'd thought themselves

Immune to arrows. The pernicious shafts
Soon took a deadly toll, and slew almost
Half of their screaming men. The arrows burned
Within their breasts, and guts, and heads, as blood
Flooded from ghastly wounds. They all cried out
With groans, as slowly and in pain they died.

Anopheles, in shock at the turn of
Events, then yelled to his men aloud with zeal:
Charge! and thus close the space between our lines,
That we may smite them with our spears and swords.
Forthwith he ran ahead of his troops, inspiring
Their will to fight. The feet of his comrades
Did roar, as close behind they charged headlong.
Stampeding cattle make such thund'rous noise.
Anopheles-- within spear range-- taunted
The Leukocytes, demeaning them with words
Of wrath: Ye pusillanimous men, who
Afar do stand and loft thy loathsome darts,
Now feel the steel of my unyielding spear!
Without delay he hurled the shaft, as fast
As falcons dive upon their prey below.
Hepatis-- young and brave-- boldly stood fast,
Awaiting the approaching horde, his shield
Before his bulk: into the buckler's bronze
Anopheles' forbidding spear did sink,
And passed on through its three bull's hide layers;
It pierced his breastplate cleanly, sank into
His stomach, and lodged within his spine.
The warrior fell with moan's of fading life,

And bit the ground, before black death compassed
His sight. As when a tree of lofty height
Is struck by fiery lightning, and crashes
To th'earth, its limbs bouncing upon impact,
So did Hepatis fall before his peers.

Racing across the battlefield, just steps
Behind his stout commander, Falcipar
Then threw his spear which soared toward the shield
Coronarus did hold. Although it skipped
Off of the bronze, it sunk into the groin
Of nearby Renalus, and spilled his blood,
As life did flee his silent, fallen form.
As though the lance had struck his throat, without
A sound he laid there breathing his last draughts.

Losing such loved comrades enraged the host
Of Leukocytes, who held their line and formed
A tight, unflinching phalanx, digging toes
Into the ground. They thrust their long lances,
Stabbing at foremost fighters: these clanged on
Armor, and shields, and pierced exposed flesh
With horrific effect. Like meat into
A grinder, rows and rows of troops perished
As stubbornly they pushed forward in waves.

Anopheles still stood blocking the blows;
His mind intent on breaking through their line
To fight his foes up close-- his two-handed,
Massive, and razor-sharp broadsword he hoped

To wield. He'd pulled his spear from Hepatis,
And now he prodded hard between the shields
To find a vulnerable target, but
He found his struggling fruitless, kindling
His ire. His eyes glowed red beneath his bronze
Helm, which was topped with a crest of awful spikes;
Upon his shoulders, lion's skin was draped;
His shield was huge, and bossed with Scylla's
Image-- her gruesome teeth were littered with
The rotting bodies of hapless sailors,
Who'd sailed too close to'er grot, in fear of cruel
Charybdis' gluttonous gorging of brine;
Most strikingly, his breastplate and his greaves
Were gleaming orichalcum, graved with fine
And detailed filigree quite intricate.

Screams and the clash of arms echoed all 'round
Anopheles, as his Malarial
Companions fell to spears of baneful wood.
Their viscous blood did swamp the roseate
Aortal cavern. Strong Sporozorus
Beside him stood, thrusting with his spear,
When Joshua sent a shaft flying fast
Toward his face. He saw it soar, and just
In time he raised his shield in vain: it passed
Clean through, and struck his helm, which it also
Did pierce with ease, then bored on through his brain
And through the back of his helm, but didn't stop until
Into Merozorus' shoulder it sank
And struck his scapula, loosing his limbs.

The two then fell together, as their threads
Of life were cut at once. Filling their steads,
Stephensius and strong Gambiaeus
Did move into the foremost ranks of men.
Anopheles continued fighting hard,
And with his spear he cut Coronarus'
Right arm: the lance did gouge into the flesh
Just as Coronarus stabbed at him with
A wrathful jab. In pain he drew on back,
And sought Sagacius, who dressed his wound
With herbal ointment, numbing the sharp pain,
And staunching fast the flow of dark-red blood.

Meanwhile, assaying his mettle, Paul threw
His spear, which found its mark, and plunged into
Tiberius' breastplate below his right
Nipple, and cleaved apart his liver's lobes,
Which sent him gasping to the ground, groaning
In agony. As when a buffalo
Is clawed by clinging lions, and it moans
In dire distress, in pain, yet refusing
To fall and die: so did Tiberius
With staggering delay his clanging fall.

Anopheles had seen his comrade's death,
And fearing outright massacre, ordered
His troops aloud: Fall back in swift retreat!

At that, his men did run, and swift-thrown spears
Rained down about them. Then, in hot pursuit

Paul ran with Joshua: they slew foes with
Their swords, their blades slashing madly into
The former vanguard now rereward. The host
Of Leukocytes followed those two (who were
The swiftest of the pack). Sunder Paul hacked
The fleeing troops, who fell in pieces 'fore
His feet. He first did smite Bellatorus,
Who stumbled as he ran, and fell unto
All fours: he swung his sword like a golf club
Between Bellatorus' long legs, thus sliced
On through the whole length of his spine, and cleaved
Apart his jaw and skull. His helm popped-off
His cloven head undamaged, as his guts and brains
And blood Poured out upon the ground. Next, Paul
Brought down his blade onto the collarbone
Of Cruzius' left arm: the steel passed through
His chest, emerging from his right armpit.
His head and arm went flying off, and blood
Sprayed from the wound.

As Paul pursued the enemy and hacked
Away, abreast to him Joshua ran,
And also swung his steel furiously.
He struck off the helmed heads of Nilius
And Clavigar with one swing of his blade;
Approaching Hyrcanus, he smote his waist,
And split him in twain. As Letifer did
Run, he almost outpaced the swift chase of
The son of Nun, but fell as that long sword
Sliced off his heel and then removed his head.

The fleeing host was headed t'ward The Heart,
And quickly neared the Aortic one-way
Valve. There the Leukocytes did corner them,
And pressed toward the last Malarial
Soldiers. They formed an arched phalanx, stabbing
With spears, and pushing onward with their shields.
They killed all but Anopheles, who held
His weighty shield and waved his lengthy lance,
And kept them all at bay. He saw he had
No hope to win the fight, and hurled his shaft
With all his strength. As soon as it thus left
His hand, the men stepped back and watched it fly,
Preparing for its strike; Anopheles
Then ran full-speed toward the cavern's curved
Wall; as his spear pierced through Splenicius'
Breastplate, and knocked him off his feet, taking
His life, Anopheles did climb the curve,
And with a spiraling egress, above
Their ranks he ran, escaping t'ward The Legs.
They turned in haste to chase, to no avail.

Chapter 3

The Leukocyte's then gathered up their dead
Comrades, and hauled them to The Nose. They brought
Them from The Nose's capillaries, out
Into The Nasal Cavity, and to
The Pharynx's pit. There they said a short prayer,
And to the acid depths of The Stomach
They sent their fallen brethren one by one.
Returning to the capillaries, back
They hurried through the vessels, to the huge
Aortal cavern, to regroup, and plan
Their search throughout The Body, to find
And then dispatch latent Anopheles.

They reached the former battlefield, and planned
To split up into companies. Before
They could depart however, four large men
The troops descried: these came into the cave
By way of The Aortal Valve. As they

25

Approached, their massive size became more clear.
Giants they were, and twice as tall as any of
The Leukocytes. Behind the four, walked bold
Anopheles, who held his spear and shield,
And wore his fearsome sword upon his back.
The giants armed themselves with pikes that looked
To be almost double the length of spears
The Leukocytes were wont to see their foes
Brandish. Their ponderous, sharp heads were wrought
Of steel-- enough to make five normal-sized
Spear-points. They each held shields that three of the
Strongest amongst the Leukocytes couldn't
Hold up. Their armor shined-- the well polished,
Thick orichalc crinkling as they came near.
Anon, Labrancius did speak with words
That boomed: Ye puny troops have felled our ranks,
But now do face commanding men, who shall
Betimes destroy ye. Then, forthwith, two troops--
Pinealus and Pancraeas: brothers
Fighting in their first battle; young and bold--
Became enraged by his affront, and both
Approached to challenge him, running with spears
Held back prepared to throw. With speed like that
Of cats, he turned his shaft, and threw it at
The men: its bulk flew fast, though turned sideways;
Before the men could raise their shields, the ash
Did strike their faces, smashing bones to bits.
They dropped at once, their limp, unmoving limbs
Flopping on down. Labrancius hurried
To grab his weapon, turning back flying

Shafts with his shield, while grabbing the fouled wood.

Coronarus (recovered from his wound)
Then said to Paul: Let us both throw our spears
Together; thou direct thy shaft toward
His face, while I aim for his waist. We'll throw on
The count of three: ...one ...two ...three!
They hurled their darts, which flew straight at his face
And waist: he saw the shaft flying fast t'ward
His eyes, and quickly raised his shield to block
Its path: the point barely sunk into its
Plating, and then fell at his feet; he failed
Though, to regard the path'f Coronarus'
Swift dart, which punched into his breastplate, cut
Apart his stomach muscles, sliced out through
His back, and slid across the ground. The wound
Disgorged his guts and blood, and down he went
With screams so loud, they hurt the Leukocytes'
Ears. His relaxed tongue fell out of his maw,
And with a gurgling groan, his life expired.

Messeaeus then swung his shaft, which was
Thick as a weaver's beam, and hacked off the heads
Of Dermisus and Subcutis, which flew
Aloft, as spurts of blood erupted from
Their necks. He roared, began to thrust the pike,
And jabbed at troops, who wavered as his blows
Knocked at their shields. The point then stuck into
Paul's orb; he tried to pull it free, in vain:
The men abreast of Paul did grab its rim,

27

And helped to keep the giant from wrenching
It from his hands. Meanwhile, Thalamius
Loaded his thick-limbed bow, and aimed the dart
With care: he let it fly with a perfect
Release, and it took-off spiraling straight:
It struck behind his jaw, below his ear,
And huge Messeaeus came crashing down.
His blood did burble from his neck, and streamed
Across the ground, as noiselessly he died.

Anon, Sacharovus did hurl his pike,
Which cleaved on through the shield Cerebellus
Did ply: it pierced into his breastplates' bronze,
But just in time, he'd turned, escaping death.
He felt the steel as it then grazed his ribs,
And left a nick which bled but drops of blood.
Enraged, Cerebellus did heave his lance,
Which lodged in th'awesome shield of hideous
Sacharovus, who plucked it from the orb,
And stabbed at foremost men with fervent thrusts.
Anopheles beside him stood, and jabbed
Away. Sergentius then lunged his shaft,
Which hit Brachialus' exposed left knee:
The massive point disjoined his lower leg,
And moaning he collapsed, and bled his life
Away. He stabbed again and drove the point
Into Tibialus' helmed head, and flung
The skewered man across the cave, dashing
Him 'gainst the wall. The beast was raging-- foam
Forming around his mouth; his eyes aglow.

He brought his shaft down on the helm of tall
Peroneus, and crushed his neck; forthwith
He swung it at Coronarus, who ducked:
Its tip then sliced the throat of Ulnarus,
Who flailed about, soaking the troops with blood.
From a distance, Thalamius aimed well once more,
And sent a winged dart into the thigh
Of great Sergentius, who snapped the shaft
And left the head within his leg. He shrugged
Away the pain, as does a lion stuck
With darts: encircled, hunters threatening with spears,
He roars and ramps, determined to fight 'til death:
So did his rage increase, as 'round him troops
Brandished their bristling spears. Again, bending
The creaking wood, Thalamius took aim,
And shot a dart into his neck: his head
Then flopped forward, as sinews snapped before
The wedge. As sunflowers burdened by seeds
Do bow their heavy heads, so did his head
Bow down, as death came swiftly over him.

Only Sacharovus and bloodthirsty
Anopheles remained. They yelled fierce cries
Of battle, jabbed in haste, and blocked hard blows.
Now, Joshua did reach behind his shield
And drew his sling out from a hidden pouch,
In which he also kept three round river
Pebbles. Into the sling he placed a smooth
Missile, and spun it 'round above his head.
He flung the stone with perfect aim: it sunk

Into Sacharovus' forehead, and brought
The monster to the ground. He twitched, and kicked,
As slaughtered cattle struck betwixt the eyes
May do, although they've lost all sensation.
As men defended Joshua, he drew
His shining blade, and smote the beast's head off.

Anopheles then stood alone, and heaved
His spear: however, th'effort seem'd hindered,
And to his horror, th'ashen shaft fell short.
Unsheathing his huge sword, he tried to charge,
But as in dreams, when fleeing from demise,
The heavy steps do slow, and weak muscles
Requite no input: so his steps did seem.

Forthwith, as Paul observed his slow advance,
He charged inflamed: his sword in hand, he cried
A fiercely pealing battle cry, swiftly
Approached Anopheles, and brought his steel
Down on his helm: the blade sundered his head
And neck and trunk, which split apart, like logs
Will do when struck well with an axe. The halves
Dropped down, and viscera fell in a heap.

Chapter 4

The troops rejoiced, as victory was theirs.
Betimes however, wearily they hauled
The dead on through The Nose, and to the pit
Where they were wont to send their fallen men.
There Joshua, in woe, did say a prayer:
Today we've won this bloody strife, because
Thou gave us strength, and armed us for battle.
For that we will be thankful all our days.
Please Lord, continue aiding us in wars
To come, and comfort us, bereft of loved
Comrades, as we commit them to the deep.
Vouchsafe to grant us wisdom-- most useful
Weapon of war-- in future fights, that we
May vanquish foes who'll try to take this realm.
We mark the day Thou helped us rout the host
Of foul Pneumonic men: forever we
Are grateful. Influenzal troops have fought
Us here in many wars, and by thy grace

We've smote each host with our relentless steel.
Thanks be to Thee oh Lord, for these vict'ries.

After they'd sent the dead down to th'acid,
The Leukocytes repaired back to the vast
Aortal cave, to hold funeral games,
In honor of the dead. In shot put, boxing,
A race on foot, and archery they would
Compete. As he was in command, Joshua
Did host th'events. He 'ppointed th'orichalc
Giants' off-stripped armor to he who proved
The best in each contest. Shot put was first:
The men discussed who would compete, and urged
Thalamius to try his might. He stood,
And joined the other men: Cerebellus,
Saphenius and Sacralus (who was
Still young, although he was quite strong). Lifting
A shot, Sacralus thus began: he heaved
The ball with awesome strength, and sent it far.
The men were well-impressed by his attempt.
Thinking themselves to have no chance to win,
Saphenius and brave Cerebellus
Then opted out, and took their seats, to watch
Thalamius-- known for his strength and wit.
He grabbed a bigger ball, and spun around:
With ease he tossed the weight beyond the spot
Sacralus' shot had lit. Proudly he took
Labranchius' armor, and sat back down.

The next event they held was foot racing.

They planned their course: they'd start at The
Aortic Valve, and run down to The Left
Arteria Renalis, through The Ren,
And through The Renal Vein; from there they'd race
On to The Heart; next they'd pass through The Lungs,
Back to The Heart, and finally, out through
Th'Aortic Valve to complete the race.
The swiftest men then stood to vie with one
Another. Young Sacralus stood, as did
Paul, swift Cerebellus, and Plantarus.
Raising a banner, Joshua signaled
For them to get ready to run, then dropped
His arm, thus sending them darting from thence.
Plantarus bolted off the line, flying
Ahead of th'others. Staying right behind
Him, quick Cerebellus gave chase, nearly
Stepping on his sandals. Behind him ran
Sacralus; Paul took up the rear, although
Almost abreast of the young contestant.
As near the half-way point they came, Paul then
Began to pass Sacralus, though he fought
To stay with Paul with dogged zeal. Passing
On through The Lungs, Sacralus once again
Outstripped the pace of Paul, and came close to
Passing Cerebellus, before he slipped
And fell. Plantarus still did keep his lead,
As to The Heart they came a second time;
Cerebellus ahead of Paul. Before
He reached Th'Aortic Valve, fleet Plantarus
Twisted his ankle, sending him down to

The ground. The twain passed by as he hopped up,
And limped on through the valve, barely beating
Sacralus. Taking th'honorable win,
Cerebellus then choose Sacharovus'
Splendidly wrought armor to be his prize.

Next, Joshua declared it time to box.
Forthwith, the best boxers stood up to fight:
Coronarus and stout Thalamius
Prepared their fists with gauntlets, layered thick--
Their leather stiff with steel. Wise Joshua
Checked to ensure that each man's were the same:
Approving, he began the fight. The men
Did cheer the fighters on, who skipped about,
Nimbly hopping on their toes, jabbing
With hasty blows. They held their fists before
Their heads, which each pulled back to thwart the strikes
The other threw. Thalamius soon struck
A blow which sent Coronarus off of
His feet. As Joshua then helped him up,
He watched his eyes, which seem'd to search about,
And wisely called the fight, declaring strong
Thalamius the winner of the clash.
Coronarus-- with rills of blood flowing
Down from his lip-- returned to sit, as proud
Thalamius received Messeaeus'
Shiny, resplendent armor as his purse.

The final contest-- Archery-- required
The contestants to shoot a dart, and as

34

If threading needles, send it through the holes
Behind the blades of twelve battle axes
Set in a line: the first who did would win.
Thus, Joshua then prudently stretched out
A string, and 'ligned the stands in which he set
The wooden shafts. He made two rows, and picked
Two bows unstrung, of equal size, to be
Those used. Anon, Thalamius stood up,
As did Cerebellus-- the men best known
For skill with bows. They took their places 'fore
The rows, and waited for the sign to start.
Seeing they were ready, Joshua
Then waved his flag. Both men were strong, and had
No trouble bending th'inelastic wood;
They finished stringing th'arms at the same time.
Cerebellus was first to shoot his dart:
It squeaked on through the sixth hole, but it struck
The seventh axe's steel. Thalamius
Forthwith did send his shaft on through all twelve
Axes, without the fletchings grazing steel
Or wood. The men applauded him, as he
Gladly accepted huge Sergentius'
Undamaged orichalc, and held it high.
Thus thrice he'd won, and slain two brutes before
His deadly bow; hence he gratefully bowed
His head, and with a prayer, he praised The Lord.

Chapter 5

Abruptly Paul awoke, confused and all
Alone. The sun was on the rise, and birds
Did sing their morning songs, as dewdrops dried
On sparkling leaves. Amazingly, to Paul's
Delight, he felt just fine and cured of his
Disease. He collected himself, and stood;
Looking this way and that, he saw no sign
Of where the Shaman went. He grabbed his pack,
And walked along the path, heading the same
Direction he had trod the day before.
A cooling breeze rustled the trees and shrubs
Below. A patch of *Phragmipediums*
Quivered beside the trail; their long, wavy
Petals did hang, drooping below their round
And shining pouches. Above the patch,
A flock of squawking parrots roosted in
A brazil nut tree, which towered over
The forest floor-- its top one hundred and

Fifty some feet above the ground. Nearby,
He saw an agouti dive into the
Dense brush, like the lizards which frequently
Scattered as he approached. He looked to find
A fallen fruit with nuts, but found only
The foraged, empty shells. Further along,
A narrow, cleared, and straightly constructed
Pathway athwart the trail was teeming with
A host of fierce leafcutter ants, which seem'd
To hold in hand a tree's worth of cut leaves.
Toward their nest they took the leaves for them
To use to fuel their fungal fodder farms.

As time passed by, Paul wondered if he would
Return back home. He put the thought out of
His mind, and tried to stay upbeat and think
Of how to find his way out of the dark
And lonely forest. Butterflies and moths
Fluttered about, as if they knew he couldn't
Expend his strength to try to catch insects.
He pressed ahead, as th'air grew hot and still
Beneath the midday sun. He was almost
Out of the water which his bottle held,
When there before his eyes he saw a leaf
Of *Heliconia* upon the ground,
About the length of his arm span, and filled
With precious rain water. He carefully
Funneled the water, filling his canteen,
Then placed a disinfecting tab within.
Relieved, he then regained his pace, instilled

With hope he would survive to find his way
Back to civilization. Hiking on,
He saw a dying tree that was the home
Of hundreds of bromeliads, which clung
Onto its bark, enjoying goodly light
Because the tree lacked a dense canopy.
High in its stocky limbs, a spectacled
Bear clung: it happily was eating rich
Hearts of bromeliads, chomping away.

He moved along, and as the sun began
To set, he saw a *Monstera* plant on
A tree beside the trail, which bore ripe fruit.
Its large and holey leaves concealed the long
And narrow, strangely patterned fruits, which smelled
Like bananas and pineapples combined.
He ate a few ripe treats, using his knife
To cut away their scaly flesh. As there
He ate that wholesome fruit, the night approached
Apace, and so he built a fire and raised
His tent. He couldn't verify what type
Of wood he found to burn, but thought it smelled
Harmless enough. While he then sat watching
The flames, the smoke began to make him feel
A strange sensation. Soon he thought the fire
Was causing it, and moved to 'void the smoke.
Howbeit, 'twas too late, and time slowed down,
As all around him sounds of creatures grew
Increasingly louder, and rhythmic'ly
They merged and formed a dreadful din.

It echoed loudly in his mind, until
He couldn't well distinguish thoughts from sounds.
Although the sun was down, the forest 'bout
Him waxed more vivid. Objects seem'd to move
In his periphery, and as he'd chase
Them with his eyes, he'd find but simple plants.
Disturbing thoughts assailed his mind, but weren't
Coherent: Poisoned? Fire? These glints of fear
Would come and go, as 'round him crickets creaked,
While frogs did chirp, and bats sent squeaks about.
He tried to rest his eyes, but found more sights
Within his lids, than he could see without.
Awake he stayed as time passed slowly on,
And weary he became, though not sleepy.
The night was coming to an end, when he
At last did fall asleep, and deeply snoozed.

Chapter 6

As Paul then slept, he slipped into a dream.
He looked up t'ward th'empyrean and saw
A distant light approaching swiftly through
Th'ethereal air. As the light came near,
He soon descried the outline of a man,
Who glowed as though he was a star-- blinding
Was th'awesome glare about his form. He wore
A flowing scarlet robe, and 'round his neck
Compassed a golden chain. He softly lit
Without the use of wings, beside where Paul
Did stand agape, and spoke: Foolishly, thou
Ignored the words of Michael, sent by God
To visit thee. So soon thou did forget
His admonition, and dismissed the will
Of God. Hast thou forgotten 'bout the men
Who scared away your guide? Dost thou now see
That they were jackals? Death may soon threaten

To seize thee once again: do heed the words
God deigned to send by way of Michael's tongue.
Exulting in success, and sorrowing
In troubling times, thou fail to see the sway
Of God. By His decree do triumphs come
To those who are His humble suppliants;
Likewise, distress and pain may come to those
Who turn their backs on Him, thinking themselves
To hold the reigns of destiny. Though free
To do thy will, thou can't escape God's sight
Upon thy path in life. When good does come
Thy way, do thank The Lord, lest thou should be
Too proud of thy own deeds: against His will,
No good can come to man. When trouble finds
Thee on thy path, do pray for help from God,
That he may take away thy woes: against
His will no harm can come to man. When life
Is uneventful, pray to God, lest things
Should fall apart, and suffering take hold:
Do not forget that all could soon turn ill.

When Thou did fail to understand the words
Which Michael spake, thou should have prayed to gain
Wisdom to grasp their meaning. Long ago,
The king of Babylon did dream a dream
That wracked his mind, though it was but a blur.
Anon, he asked the wise, the soothsayers,
The sorcerers, and magicians to shew
Him what he'd seen, and to elucidate
Its meaning. Death he'd give to all those men,

If none could shew the king his dream and what
It meant. I was amongst the wise, yet was
Befuddled 'bout the dream, and feared swift death.
Therefore, I prayed to know just what he'd dreamt,
And the interpretation. God then sent
To me a vision of the image he had seen:
A man of gold, silver, bright brass, iron,
And clay, that fell beneath a stone, cut from
A mountain side-- though not by human hands--
Which crushed and turned the strange figure to dust.
God also shewed the meaning thereof; thus,
I told the king what he desired to hear,
And that there is a God above who'd deigned
To shew the thing to me because I'd prayed.
So, by the grace of God the king did spare
My life. If thou had prayed about thy dream
And Michael's solemn words, The Lord would've
Shewn thee forthwith His message's meaning.

My faith has saved me more than once from harm.
During the reign of Darius, I faced
A grisly death, but God protected me.
I ruled above the king's princes
And presidents, and held the favor of
The king. In time, those gov'nors sought to bring
Me down. They watched my ev'ry move to find
A fault by which I broke the law, but none
Was found. Thus, they plotted against me. Since
'Twas known I prayed each day, they sought to make
My prayers a breach of law. Unto the king

Those wicked men did bring a document
To sign: it was a statute saying that no man
Except the king could ask petition-- not
Of any God or man-- for thirty days:
Whoever acted 'gainst the signed decree,
The king would cast into the lions' den.
I knew the king had done their will and signed
The document, yet even so I prayed
Three times per day. The gov'nors saw that I
Still prayed, and went unto the king and said:
Hast thou not signed a decree saying that
No one shall ask petition of any
God or of any man for thirty days,
And that transgressors shall be cast into
The lions' den? The king replied: It's true,
According to the Medes' and Persians'
Law, which does not allow alteration.
The men then told the king: Daniel does not
Regard your word, as still he prays three times
A day. At this the king became greatly
Displeased he'd signed the words into effect.
He sought to change the law, to save me from
That fate, but firmly, those vile men informed
The king: The law of the Medes and of
The Persians stays the king from changing signed
Decrees. At last the king submitted to
Their wish: they brought me to the lions' den,
And to the beasts they dropped me. Looking down
Into the lair, the king then said in hope:
Thy god thou praise unfailingly, he will

Deliver thee from harm. I gazed into
The sunlit sky, as o'er the mouth they slid
A heavy stone, then stared about into
The dark, and saw the stately beasts: one stood
To calmly stretch its legs, while others couched
And licked their lips. Another snored with deep
Rumbles, which made the hair stand on my skin.
I asked The Lord to shut the lions' mouths,
And sat against the wall, faithful that He
Would keep me safe. As silently I sat,
I heard the gurgling groan of a hungry
Stomach: a quite unpleasant sound to hear.
I calmed my thoughts, and kept them calm, until
Around the early morning hours, when fear
Did strike my heart: a sleeping lion groaned
As dreams disturbed its mind. I jumped, but then
I saw that it was lying there asleep,
And soon I knew the slumb'ring beast had meant
No harm. As dawn approached, the lions slept,
And I remained unscathed. The king awoke
Betimes, forthwith repaired unto the den,
And told his men: Remove the stone which seals
The mouth. He peered into the dark, and called
With mournful words: Daniel! Thy god thou praise
Unfailingly, praying toward the west
Three times a day, is he able to save
Thou from the lions? Gladly I replied:
O king, unto the ages may you live:
The Lord did shut the lions mouths, and I
Am yet unharmed. The king was greatly pleased,

And ordered men to pull me from the lair.
They lowered me a rope, and drew me up.
By God's decree I came up from that pit
Unscathed: the next to touch the den's cool floor
Were torn to shreds. Thou must also seek God's
Succor, to safely find your way out of
The forest. Thou'll soon face a deadly threat,
And stray the wrong direction. Pray unto
The Lord: thy light of hope may soon grow dim,
If thou should fail to see thou need His help.

There is another issue that The Lord
Has sent me here to speak about to you:
As humans learn how life is formed, ye see
How beautifully formed it is. Thou art
A scientist, and understand divers
Complexities of life; therefore, more so
Thou should appreciate the perfect plan
That God contrived; howbeit, thou art but
Impressed by man's deciphering of how
The many processes of life perform.
The Lord does find thy viewpoint impious.
Revere the Lord's designs, because they are
The greatest artistry there'll ever be.

Paul stood in awe, with questions racing through
His mind. He couldn't speak, as Daniel turned
And flew away towards the firmament.
He soared so fast, it seem'd as though he was
A distant glimmer the instant he left.

Chapter 7

The sun already lit the canopy
Above his tent, when perched nearby in a
Tree fern, a Tanager of Paradise
Erupted into song, with chirps and high
Screeches that filled the air. Its head and chest
Light-green and blue, its back and rump jet-black
And red, it gaily squealed as if to wake
Up Paul, who opened up his tent to see
The noisy bird. As hunger wrenched his gut,
He packed his gear, and then set off along
The trail. Anon, across the path at eye
Level, a branch did droop, and on its twigs
There stood a long and slender stick insect:
Its camouflage almost enough to fool
His eyes. The creature swayed and slowly crept,
As Paul beneath him ducked his head, and moved
On. Now, the trail became a narrow pass,
Along a crag that hung over a vale.

He saw a trickling stream below, that seem'd
To flow out from the rocky face under
His feet, and looking on, he saw a route
To use to reach the valley floor. Gazing
Up through the opened canopy above,
He saw but thick, white clouds, and found no hope
To see the sun. He thought it best to make
His way on down, and walk along the stream,
To follow it in hope that it would flow
Into a larger water course, and lead
Him to a village. Slowly, he then climbed
On down the route he'd seen, and reached the place
Where from the rock the water sprang. He poured
The water out from his canteen, and filled
It with the clear supply. He placed a tab
Within, and walked along the curvy stream.
The forest there was dense and dark, and soon
He saw upon his path a ghastly sight:
A human skull. Recoiling, he gripped
His spear with white knuckles, and prepped
His knife, unbuckling the strap that held
It in its sheath. His pace increased, and then
Forthwith, he thought about his dream, and prayed
To God: Although I've failed to look to You
O Lord, I now do hope to find Your love,
That You might take me 'neath Your wing,
And show me safely from this baleful place.
Please Lord, forgive me for my lack of faith;
Please shelter me from harm and guide me home.

He walked in consternation, glancing left
And right, as thoughts of toothy beasts beset
His mind. As he then looked about, but not
At where he placed his feet, a Fer-de-Lance
Did cross his path: he almost stepped right on
The serpent's back, but just before he touched
Its scaly coat, he saw the trapezoids
Upon its scales moving along, drew back
His foot, and leapt as though he were a frog;
Over the deadly threat he soared, and watched
It slither through the brush. Though scared,
He now did walk with greater care beside
The stream. The plants grew thick around his path:
He couldn't see beyond the growth that flanked his steps,
And felt as though something was watching him.
On edge he walked, and listened as he tried
To keep from crunching leaves fallen before
His feet. A rustling startled him, and as
He turned with spear in hand, he saw what made
The noise: a large iguana darting through the bush;
However, that very moment, a fierce
Jaguar exploded from the green, reaching
At him with hooking claws: but as it jumped,
Its paw did land upon his lance. It yelped
In pain, and ran away with haste, as Paul
Fled fast in fear downstream with springing steps.

The growth about the stream became less dense,
And Paul soon stopped to catch his breath. He then
Remembered how that lizard saved him from

The jaguar's silent ambush: wherefore, he
Gladly did thank The Lord. He thought about
The snake he'd almost stepped right on, and slowed
His pace. Now, looking down, he saw a mat
Of amethyst slime mold growing upon
The leafy bank, and guessed it was unknown
To science. Moving on, he saw a white,
Yellow, and purple *Cattleya*, fixed to
The bark of an old tree: a stunning sight
Indeed. Its frilly petals seem'd like wings
Above its brightly-colored, robe-like lip.

As lonely hours did slowly pass, and day
Gave way to ev'ning's dimming glow, he trudged
Along exhausted, thinking that he'd set
Up camp as soon as he could find a spot
To raise his tent. Athwart his path, the wind
Was steadily blowing, and had done so
Most of the afternoon. Then, to his delight,
He caught a scent of cooking. Thrilled, he turned
Toward the smell, and paced with growing hope,
As stronger grew the fragrance with each step.
He finally descried a distant plume
Of smoke, and ran with joy. As he approached
He heard the sound of children's playful screams,
And knew at last he'd make it home alive.
He staggered from the brush, dizzy from lack
Of food, and on his meager countenance
The villagers did set their wond'ring eyes.
At once a man addressed him in Spanish,

And told him he should sit and join them for
The meal they had prepared, and stay the night.

Chapter 8

At dawn a cock'rel crowed, and Paul awoke
Within his tent: relieved to know he'd soon be home,
He'd slept in perfect peace, and felt refreshed.
Serg, one of the Spanish speaking locals,
Who'd proffered that he'd guide him back to La
Chorrera, then awoke and met him with
Some fried plantains to eat before they hiked.

Paul packed his tent, and left with Serg to make
The fifteen-mile journey. They strode along
The lushly verdant trail, as children yelled
Goodbyes. The morning air was calm, and fog
Still lingered 'bove the undergrowth. Though Paul's
Mind was now set on going home, he still
Was 'mazed by all the forest life. Serg stopped
And pointed at a leaf: he looked, and saw
A group of eggs, beside a pair of glass
Frogs: their translucent bodies let the green

Show through from under them, hiding their forms.
As Paul then stared, he saw a Blue-and-Gold
Macaw, that climbed upon a tree using
Its beak and claws. They trudged along on up
A hill, and when they reached its peak, they saw
Two Andean *Rupicola*, with orange
Shoulders and heads, and black and charcoal chests
And tails, that squabbled on a branch to win
A female. Briefly, they stopped there to watch,
Then moved along amused.   The mid-morn heat
Was 'ssuaged by pleasant gusts of cooling wind,
And cheerful birds were calling all around.
Paul saw a tiny, green moth, with a spot
On either wing. It was the size of a
Thumbnail, and blended with the leaf on which
It sat. He knew it was a species of
Rosema. Pacing on, he left it there
Unhurt. Anon, they smelled a strong fetid
Odor, and there before them was a patch
Of tall *Dracontium* plants, blooming with
Their purple spathes that stunk of rotting flesh.
Around them flies were buzzing, 'ttracted to
The stench. Their spreading leaves were held
Aloft by blotchy petioles, that matched
Their flowers' stretching peduncles.
A breeze began to blow the odious
Odor toward the men, and speedily
They moved along. Now, Paul espied a group
Of small *Pinguicula* carnivorous
Plants, which had flies stuck to their leaves,

And flowers that bobbed with blue petals, on stalks
Above their foliage. As they walked on,
Serg said that they were getting close to La
Chorrera. Paul thought back on all he'd seen
And felt within the forest's depths, and all
He'd learned. Those thoughts continued when they reached
The town, and stayed with him as back he flew
To Bogota, and as he flew back home.

I'd heard my Dad's completed tale, and prayed
That night that God would be my guide through life.
I woke up early the next morn, and with
My Mom and Dad I drove down to the docks,
Where I then met up with my eager crew.
Together there we prayed for our safe trip,
And then toward the rising sun we sailed.